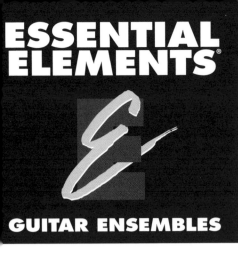

ESSENTIAL ELEMENTS

GUITAR ENSEMBLES

JIMI HENDRIX®

CONTENTS

Arrangements by Chip Henderson and Chad Johnson
Cover photo: Torben Dragsby / © Authentic Hendrix, LLC
Songs and lyrics by Jimi Hendrix, © Experience Hendrix, L.L.C. All Rights Reserved.

ISBN 978-1-4584-0086-4

EXCLUSIVELY DISTRIBUTED BY

7777 W. BLUEMOUND RD. P.O. BOX 13819 MILWAUKEE, WI 53213

Visit Hal Leonard Online at
www.halleonard.com

ALL ALONG THE WATCHTOWER

Words and Music by Bob Dylan

CASTLES MADE OF SAND

Words and Music by Jimi Hendrix

CROSSTOWN TRAFFIC

Words and Music by Jimi Hendrix

FIRE

Words and Music by Jimi Hendrix

FOXEY LADY

Words and Music by Jimi Hendrix

FREEDOM

Words and Music by Jimi Hendrix

HEY JOE

Words and Music by Billy Roberts

I DON'T LIVE TODAY

Words and Music by Jimi Hendrix

LITTLE WING

Words and Music by Jimi Hendrix

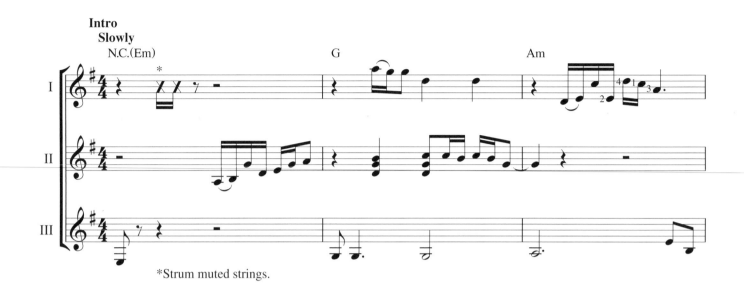

*Strum muted strings.

MANIC DEPRESSION

Words and Music by Jimi Hendrix

Intro
Moderately fast

*Strum muted strings.

Verse

PURPLE HAZE

Words and Music by Jimi Hendrix

SPANISH CASTLE MAGIC

Words and Music by Jimi Hendrix

THIRD STONE FROM THE SUN

Words and Music by Jimi Hendrix

VOODOO CHILD (SLIGHT RETURN)

Words and Music by Jimi Hendrix

THE WIND CRIES MARY

Words and Music by Jimi Hendrix

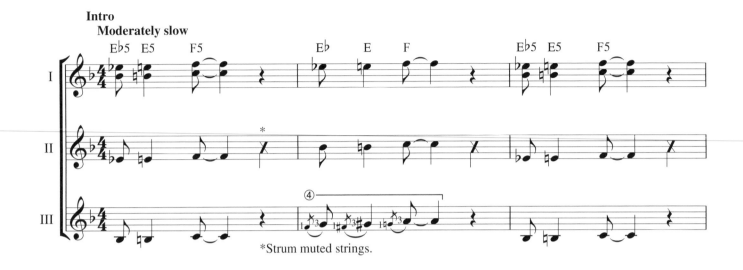

*Strum muted strings.

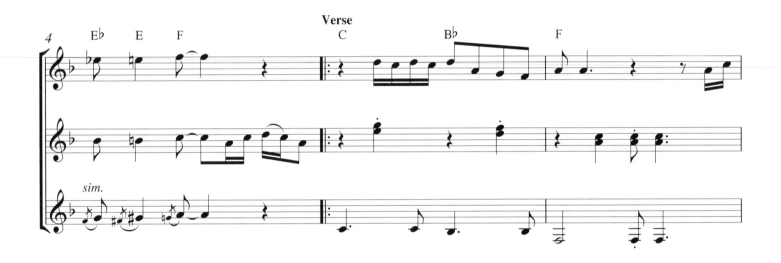

ESSENTIAL ELEMENTS FOR GUITAR

Comprehensive Guitar Method
by Will Schmid and Bob Morris

Take your guitar teaching to a new level! With the time-tested classroom teaching methods of Will Schmid and Bob Morris, popular songs in a variety of styles, and quality demonstration and backing tracks on the accompanying CD, *Essential Elements for Guitar* is a staple of guitar teachers' instruction – and helps beginning guitar students off to a great start.

This method has been designed to meet the National Standards for Music Education, with features such as cross-curricular activities, quizzes, multicultural songs, basic improvisation and more. Concepts covered in Book 1 include: getting started; basic music theory; guitar chords; notes on each string; music history; ensemble playing; performance spotlights; and much more!

Songs used in Book 1 include such hits as: Dust in the Wind • Eleanor Rigby • Every Breath You Take • Hey Jude • Hound Dog • Let It Be • Ode to Joy • Rock Around the Clock • Stand by Me • Surfin' USA • Sweet Home Chicago • This Land Is Your Land • You Really Got Me • and more!

00862639 Book/CD Pack $17.99

Essential Elements Guitar Ensembles

The songs in the Essential Elements Guitar Ensemble series are playable by three or more guitars. Each arrangement features the melody, a harmony part, and bass line in standard notation along with chord symbols. For groups with more than three or four guitars, the parts can be doubled. This series is perfect for classroom guitar ensembles or other group guitar settings.

THE BEATLES
Early Intermediate Level
Can't Buy Me Love • Day Tripper • Hey Jude • Penny Lane • and more.
00865008 .... $9.99

BOSSA NOVA
Intermediate/Advanced Level
Desafinado • The Girl from Ipanema • Little Boat • Wave • and more.
00865006 .... $9.99

CHRISTMAS SONGS
Mid-Beginner Level
The Christmas Song • Frosty the Snowman • Jingle-Bell Rock • Rudolph the Red-Nosed Reindeer • and more.
00001136 .... $9.95

POP HITS
Late Beginner Level
Brown Eyed Girl • Dust in the Wind • Imagine • Oh, Pretty Woman • and more.
00001128 .... $9.99

ROCK CLASSICS
Late Beginner Level
Behind Blue Eyes • Crazy Train • Free Bird • Low Rider • Smoke on the Water • and more.
00865001 .... $9.95

CLASSICAL THEMES
Late Beginner Level
Air on the G String • Canon in D • Für Elise • Moonlight Sonata • and more.
00865005 .... $9.99

JAZZ BALLADS
Early Intermediate Level
Body and Soul • Misty • My Funny Valentine • The Nearness of You • and more.
00865002 .... $9.99

JAZZ STANDARDS
Mid-Intermediate Level
All the Things You Are • Blue Skies • Georgia on My Mind • It's Only a Paper Moon • and more.
00865007 .... $9.99

EASY POP SONGS
Mid-Beginner Level
All My Loving • The House of the Rising Sun • Lean on Me • Purple Haze • and more.
00865011 .... $9.99

Flash Cards

96 CARDS FOR BEGINNING GUITAR
00865000 .... $7.95

Essential Elements Guitar Repertoire Series

Hal Leonard's Essential Elements Guitar Repertoire Series features great original guitar music based on a style or theme that is carefully graded and leveled for easy selection. The songs are presented in standard notation and tablature, and are fully demonstrated on the accompanying CD.

TURBO ROCK
Beginner Intermediate Level
by Mark Huls
00001076 Book/CD Pack $9.95

BLUES CRUISE
Mid-Intermediate Level
by Dave Rubin
00000470 Book/CD Pack $9.95

MYSTERIOSO
Mid-Intermediate Level
by Allan Jaffe
00000471 Book/CD Pack $9.95

DAILY GUITAR WARM-UPS
by Tom Kolb
Mid-Beginner to Late Intermediate

This book contains a wide variety of exercises to help get your hands in top playing shape. It addresses the basic elements of guitar warm-ups by category: stretches and pre-playing coordination exercises, picking exercises, right and left-hand synchronization, and rhythm guitar warm-ups.
00865004 Book/CD Pack $9.99

Essential Elements Guitar Songs

The books in the Essential Elements Guitar Songs series feature popular songs specially selected for the practice of specific guitar chord types. Each book includes eight great songs and a CD with fantastic sounding play-along tracks. Practice at any tempo with the included Amazing Slow Downer software!

POWER CHORD ROCK

Mid-Beginner Level
All the Small Things • Rock You Like a Hurricane • Smells Like Teen Spirit • You Really Got Me • and more.
00001139 Book/CD Pack $12.99

OPEN CHORD ROCK

Mid-Beginner Level
Brown Eyed Girl • Have You Ever Seen the Rain? • Love Me Do • Should I Stay or Should I Go • and more.
00001138 Book/CD Pack $12.99

BARRE CHORD ROCK
Late Beginner Level
All Along the Watchtower • Born to Be Wild • Nowhere Man • Summer of '69 • and more.
00001137 Book/CD Pack $12.99

FOR MORE INFORMATION, SEE YOUR LOCAL MUSIC DEALER,
OR WRITE TO:

HAL•LEONARD®
CORPORATION
7777 W. BLUEMOUND RD. P.O. BOX 13819 MILWAUKEE, WI 53213

Prices, contents, and availability subject to change without notice.

0311